Zac's train

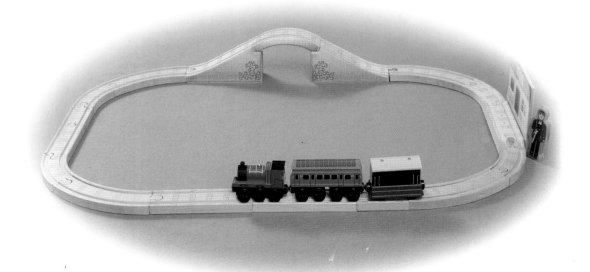

Rigby®
A Harcourt Achieve Imprint

www.Rigby.com
1-800-531-5015

Here is my train set.

3

Here are the tracks.

the

The tracks go here.

Here is the station.

The station goes here.

Here is the bridge.

The bridge goes here.

Here is the engine.

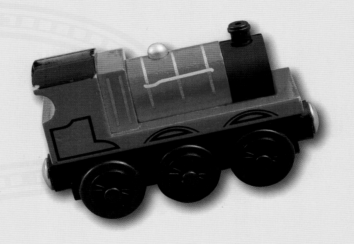

Here are the train cars.

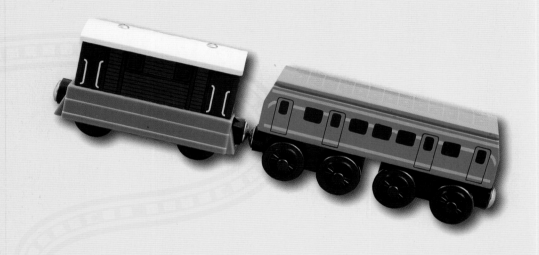

Here is the train.

Here comes the train.